OF GODS
AND
GIANTS

NORSE MYTHOLOGY

OF GODS AND GIANTS

NORSE MYTHOLOGY

BY HARALD HVEBERG

TRANSLATED BY

PAT SHAW IVERSEN

TANUM – NORLI

OSLO 1976

ISBN 82-518-0083-8

Dreyer Aksjeselskap, Stavanger

FOREWORD

The purpose of this little book is to give a concrete and clear-cut presentation of some of the ancient, well-known Norse myths.

The most important sources of Norse Mythology are the Elder (Poetic) and Younger (Prose) Eddas. The Elder Edda contains a number of poems about the gods, which have come into being in the Viking Age. The Younger Edda is, in reality, a handbook in Skaldic Poetry which was written by Snorri Sturlason around A.D. 1220. In the first section he presents the mythology in which the skalds had to be well-versed, for it was the basis of the symbolic language which they used in their poems.

The Viking Age was a warlike and restless period, and the mythology with which we have become acquainted in these two Eddas, is strongly marked by the times. It is a warrior religion in which there are many gods of war, with Odin as the highest.

On the other hand, there were many at that time who were beginning to lose their beliefs in the ancient gods. Some consoled themselves solely with their "own power and strength"; others had come so far that they believed in one God who had created heaven and earth, and ruled over everything. It cannot be precluded that these latter may have heard tidings of the God of the Christians, for many of the Germanic tribes in Middle Europe, and the Anglo Saxons in England had already embraced Christianity before the Viking Age. Nor is the Edda Mythology free from a sprinkling of Christianity. Thus, some scholars believe that Balder the Good, who, innocent and pure, suffers death but comes back after the destruction of the world, is a heathen Christ-figure. Another trend, which is no doubt due to the influence of Christianity, is that the Almighty who rules over everything shall come from above, after Ragnarok (The Twilight of the Gods), and pronounce judgement.

Harald Hveberg.

CONTENTS

The Creation

In the beginning
– – –
there was neither sand nor sea
nor cooling billows,
there was no earth
nor heaven above
– Ginnungagap was there –
and nowhere was there grass.

Thus the poem *Voluspå* (The Volve's Prophecy) describes the state of things before earth and heaven were created. To the south in this gaping void emerged *Muspellsheim* (the realm of destruction). There it was glowing hot, and no one could journey there who did not belong to this realm. *Surt,* the fire jotun, stands guard at the borders with his flaming sword, and when the end of the world comes, he will fare forth and lay waste, conquer all the *Æsir* (the gods) and burn up the whole world.

But to the north in this void lay *Nivlheim* (the realm of the mist). Here were ice and frost and fog. In the middle lay a well called *Kvergjelme,* and from it icy streams of venom ran out into Ginnungagap. Some of these streams are called *Elivågar.* When they had come so far from their source that they hardened, they turned to ice, and when the ice stopped flowing, rime formed upon it, and one layer of rime formed upon the other all the way to Ginnungagap.

But, as the northern part of Ginnungagap was filled with tremendous amounts of ice and rime, which gave forth mist and fog, so the southern end of Ginnungagap cleared from the sparks that flew from Muspellsheim. And, while everything near Nivlheim was cold and forbidding, all that lay near Muspellsheim was hot and bright, and Ginnungagap was as mild as the still air. And when the gusts of heat met the rime so that it melted and started to drip, life came into these drops from the energy of the heat, and a mighty giant, *Yme,* came into being.

As the rime continued to drip, a cow came into being. She was called *Audhumla,* and from her udders flowed four rivers of milk on which Yme was nourished.

As he slept, he started to sweat. Then from under his left arm a man and a woman emerged, while one of his feet begat a son with the other. From them are descended the *jotuns* or evil frost giants.

Audhumla licked the blocks of rime, which were salty, and on the evening of the first day the hair of a man emerged from

10

the ice, on the second day the head, and on the third day the entire man. He was called *Bure*. He was fair to look upon, and big and strong. He had a son called *Bor,* who in turn had three sons: *Odin, Vile* and *Ve*. They were fair and good, and from them are descended the Æsir, or gods.

Odin and his brothers killed Yme, and so much blood poured out of his wounds that all the jotuns were drowned save one, who, with his wife, managed to climb up into a boat. From them the new race of jotuns is descended.

The three brothers took Yme's body and placed it in the middle of Ginnungagap. From his flesh they created the earth, from his bones the mountains, from his teeth and broken knuckles the boulders and rocks, from his blood the seas and lakes and rivers, and from his hair the trees and grass. They mounted his skull high above the earth as the sky, with four corners. Under each corner they put a dwarf to hold it up, and they were called "East", "West", "North" and "South". And they scattered his brains throughout the space as clouds.

Yme's flesh was crawling with maggots. The gods gave them wits and human appearance, and they became dwarfs. They dwell under the ground and in the stones. They stay behind the mountain wall, and reply with their "dwarf tongue" (echo) whenever anyone shouts to them. They are small and ugly, but clever smiths, and no one can equal them at this. All fine weapons and precious stones were made by the dwarfs. The dwarfs hated both gods and mortals, and wanted to do them harm. When they were forced to work for them, they usually tried to make the objects in such a way that they would harm the owner.

One day, as the three Æsir were walking along the shore, they found two trees. They took them up and created Man and Woman out of them. Odin gave them breath and life, Vile gave them understanding, and Ve gave them warmth and human senses. The man was called *Ask* and the woman *Embla,* and from them are descended the mortals.

The gods also created the elves. Some are elves of light. They are good and fairer than the sun, and they live in *Alvheim.* Others are elves of darkness. They are as black as ink, and, like the dwarfs, stay beneath the earth.

Around the disk of the earth lay the deep sea, and outermost, along the shores, the evil jotuns dwelled in *Jotunheim* and *Utgard.* The jotuns were so cruel to the mortals that the Æsir took Yme's eyebrows and made a great wall around the middle part of the earth, *Midgard,* where the mortals dwelled.

From earth to heaven the Æsir raised the bridge *Bivrost* (the quivering bridge or Rainbow). It is the most magnificent and strongest bridge ever made, but one day it too shall break. The red in it is fire to keep the jotuns from crossing it into heaven.

Odin and his brothers also created the heavenly bodies. They took the sparks from Muspellsheim, which flew about in the air, and placed them in the middle of Ginnungagap, both high and low, to shine over heaven and earth. Both the sun and the moon were placed on their own chariots.

A man called *Mundilfare* had two children, and they were so radiant and fair that he named his son *Måne* (Moon), and his daughter *Sol* (Sun). But the gods were outraged by such presumption, and placed the brother and sister up in the heavens. They let Sol drive the horses which draw the chariot of the sun, and Måne was made to drive the chariot of the moon, and he rules over the waxing and the waning. Sol and Måne hurry as fast as they can, for two jotuns in wolfskins pursue them, and want to devour them. When the wolves catch up with Sol and Måne, the time for the end of the world has come.

A jotun had a daughter called *Natt* (Night), who was dark like the jotuns. She was wedded to *Delling,* the son of a god, and their son, who was light and fair, was called *Dag* (Day). Odin took Natt and Dag and placed them in the sky. He gave them each a horse and chariot, and let them drive around the earth, each in his half of the day. Natt drives first with the horse

Rimfakse (Frost Mane), and each morning dew falls upon the fields from the foam on its bridle. Afterwards, Dag drives with *Skinfakse* (the horse with the shining mane), that spreads light in the air and over the earth.

Related to the Æsir were the demigods called *Vaner*. They lived in *Vanaheim,* and ruled in particular over the powers in nature. Once there was a war between the Æsir and the Vaner, but it ended in a truce. Each took hostages from the other. The Vaner received one of the oldest of the Æsir, and the Æsir received Njord, and his children Frey and Freya.

ASGARD AND THE WORLD-TREE

In *Midgard* (middle earth), the Æsir lived in *Asgard*. There lay the meadow *Idavollen,* with Odin's throne *Lidskjalv.* When he sat on it, he could look out over the whole world, heaven and earth, and see everything that was going on. In Asgard the Æsir built a magnificent hall, *Gladsheim* (the glittering home), with thrones for Odin and the twelve highest gods. Everything there, inside and out, was of purest gold. They also built another splendid hall, *Vingolv* (the hall of friendship), for Frigg and the other goddesses. Around Lidskjalv, the Æsir built a hall which was called *Valaskjalv.* It was covered with silver. But the largest building in Asgard was Odin's banquet hall *Valhall.* There Odin held feasts for the Æsir and the fallen warriors who came to him. Valhall was so large that it had 640 doors, and 960 warriors could walk abreast through each door. The ceiling was made of spears, the roof was covered with shields, and coats of mail hung over the benches in the hall.

When the highest gods sit on the thrones in Gladsheim, they hold court. And by the ash *Yggdrasil* (the world-tree), all the Æsir meet every day and hold council. It is the largest and most magnificent tree that anyone knows of. Its evergreen branches stretch out over the whole world, and reach up above the heavens. The tree has three roots. One is with the Æsir, the second with the jotuns, and the third is over Nivlheim. Under the root over Nivlheim is a well, *Kvergjelme,* and there lies the serpent *Nidhogg,* with many other serpents, gnawing at the root. Under the root in Jotunheim there is also a well, *Mimesbrunn,* and in it is

hidden all wisdom. This well is owned by the jotun *Mime*. He knows more than anyone else, for he drinks from the well every day. One day Odin came and asked Mime for a drink, but he did not get it until he had left one of his eyes as security.

Under the third root, with the Æsir in heaven, there is also a well. It is called *Urdarbrunn,* and it is here that the gods hold their council. They ride to it over Bivrost, the quivering rainbow bridge of the Gods, between earth and heaven.

By this well there is a splendid hall. In it live three maidens, *Urd, Verdande* and *Skuld* – or Past, Present and Future. These demigoddesses, The *Norns* or the Fates, rule over the destinies of mortals, and, indeed, even over the destinies of the Æsir, and no one can change what they have decided. These are the three foremost Norns, but there are many others, some good and some evil. This is why the destinies of mortals are so different. Norns are always present whenever a child is born, and they decide its fate right away, and everything happens as they have prophesied.

In the top of Yggdrasil sits a wise eagle, and between its eyes is a hawk. Four deer eat leaves off the branches, and a squirrel runs up and down the trunk, bearing bitter words between Nidhogg and the eagle. Thus the world-tree suffers more pain than anyone is aware of. The deer bite off leaves, Nidhogg gnaws at the root, and the trunk starts rotting on the sides. Nonetheless, the tree always remains fresh and green, for each day the Norns take water from the sacred well, and pour it over the tree so that it will not rot. The water is so sacred that eveything that comes down in it turns a shining white. Beside the well, honeydew drips down to the earth from the branches of Yggdrasil, and in the well two swans are swimming about.

ODIN

Odin is the highest of the Æsir. Thus he is also called "The Father of the Universe". He rules over everything, and the other gods serve him the way children serve their father.

He has but one eye, because he has mortgaged the other eye to Mime, and he is usually thought of as a somewhat older man. Sometimes he calls himself *Hårbard* (greybeard), and he is also known as *Sidskjegg* and *Sidhatt*.

Otherwise he is strong and handsome, and he rides to battle wearing a golden helmet and coat of mail, and carrying the spear *Gungne*. It hits everything he hurls it at. On his arm he wears the ring *Draupne*. It is such that, every ninth night, eight rings drip from it, and they are just as heavy. The horse he rides upon is the grey *Sleipne* which has eight legs, and a faster horse is not to be found.

There are several gods of war, but Odin is the foremost. In Valhall (the Hall of the Fallen Warriors), Odin gathers the warriors around him and holds a feast for them. There they revel every day. In the morning at daybreak they go out, clad in their mail, and fight on the plain. But when it is getting on towards breakfast-time, the fallen warriors rise up again, and they all sit down, reconciled, to the meal. More and more warriors come. Nonetheless, there is never an end to the food in Valhall, for they live off the flesh of the boar *Særimne*. The cook, *Andrimne*, roasts it every day in the cauldron *Eldrimne*, but in the evening the boar is just as whole and alive as before. With the meat they drink ale and mead. Odin drinks only wine, and this is both food and drink for him. He gives his food to his two wolves *Gjere* and *Freke* (both meaning "the greedy"). All the mead the warriors drink pours from the udders of the goat *Heidrun,* which stands on Valhall's roof and bites branches from the tree *Lærad.* The mead runs down into a vessel which is so large that everyone has plenty to drink.

The *Valkyries* serve the warriors in Valhall. Odin also sends them out in the battle to "choose the fallen". They control who will win and who will fall in the struggle. They are called "Odin's Maidens". They are young and beautiful, and when they set out they are clad in full armor. Then they ride over the whole world, through the air and over the sea.

Odin is the god of wisdom. The others come to him when they need advice and help. He has obtained his wisdom by drinking from Mime's well. But his two ravens, *Hugin* (thought) and *Munin* (memory), also bring him information. They usually sit on his shoulders, – but every morning he sends them out into the wide world, and at breakfast-time they come flying home again and report to Odin everything they have seen. For this reason he is also called the "Raven God".

In addition, Odin is the god of skaldic poetry. In order to be a skald, he stole the skaldic mead from Suttung the jotun. How this came about, we shall hear later. He is also the god of runes. From Odin, mortals have learned both skaldic art and runecraft.

Odin has many sons. One of them is *Hermod,* whom he uses as his messenger. His surname is "the fleet", and Odin himself has given him a helmet and a coat of mail. Hermod is renowned for his trip to Hel to bring back Balder.

Wednesday gets its name from Odin.

TOR

Tor is the son of Odin and *Jord* (Earth). He is the strongest of the gods. His home is called *Trudvang,* or the "field of strength". There stands his hall, *Bilskirne* (the flashing), which has 540 rooms.

Tor is often called "The Charioteer", because he drives across the heavens in a chariot drawn by his two billygoats, *Tanngnjost* (the gnasher) and *Tanngrisne* (the gaper). When he drives, mountain tremble and crack, and the earth is scorched beneath his chariot. Then a mighty booming is heard which people call *tordönn* (or thunder).

Tor is always fighting the jotuns, and defends both gods and mortals against them. Without him, it would not have been easy for the Æsir to take care of themselves, but he always appears on the spot as soon as they mention his name.

In the struggle against the jotuns, Tor has the help of three precious objects. First there is the hammer *Mjölne* (the crusher), which the dwarfs have forged. This he can make as large or as small as he wishes. It always hits the mark when he hurls it, and comes back of its own accord. The jotuns know it well, which is not so strange as it has crushed the skulls of many of their forefathers and kinsfolk. Then he has a strength-giving belt, *Megingjord,* and when he girds it about himself, his Æsir strength is doubled. Finally, he has a pair of iron gloves which he puts on whenever he is going to use his hammer.

As far as strength is concerned, Tor is the foremost of the gods, but when it comes to word-duels, it happens that he meets his match. Then he plunges in blindly, but is not wise enough, he blunders and gets stuck completely. He can be so angry that it seems as though fire is flashing from his eyes. He is always very busy, and has little time. When the gods ride to Yggdrasil to hold their council, he never takes the time to ride over Bivrost, but takes a shortcut and comes wading through deep rivers.

Thursday gets its name from Tor.

OTHER ÆSIR

Balder is one of Odin's sons, and *Frigg* is his mother. About him there are only good things to report. He is kind and saintly, and everyone praises him. He is so fair that he shines. A flower is so white that it has been compared with Balder's eyebrows. It is called *Balderbrå* (mayweed), and it is whitest of all flowers. Balder is wise and gentle, and an eloquent speaker, and he is merciful and lenient.

He lives at *Breidablik*. Here he has his castle, and nothing unclean must be found there. He is married to Nanna.

Balder was slain by his brother Hod, but one day he shall come back again, when everything has been destroyed in Ragnarok.

Ty is also one of Odin's sons. He is the boldest of the Æsir, and he rules to some extent over the victory in the battles. Courageous men should invoke him. Ty is a war god like Odin, and the most entertaining thing he knows of is to cause strife. Never has it been heard that he has reconciled anyone. A proof of his boldness is the way he lost one of his hands. Of this we shall hear later. Tuesday (Ty's Day) gets its name from Ty.

Brage is another of Odin's sons. He is renowned for his wisdom, and even more for his eloquence, but most of all because he is a clever skald. The Vikings thought of him as an old, honorable man with a long beard. Idun is his wife.

Heimdall was born, in a miraculous manner, of nine jotun maidens who were all sisters. But some say that he is one of Odin's sons, too. He is called "the white god", and he is big and holy. He has teeth of gold, and for this reason he is also known as

Gold Tooth. His horse is called *Gulltopp*. Heimdall's dwelling is called *Himinbjorg* (the heavenly mountain), and is near Bivrost. He is the watchman of the gods, and sits here, at the edge of heaven, guarding the bridge against the mountain giants. He needs less sleep than a bird, and night and day can see a hundred miles. He can hear the grass growing in the fields, and the wool growing on the sheep. He has a lure which is called *Gjallarhorn*, and when he blows on it, it can be heard over the whole world.

Vidar is the son of Odin and the jotun woman *Grid*. He is called "the silent god". He is the next strongest after Tor, and in every emergency the gods rely upon him considerably. In the last great battle of the gods, he avenges Odin, and breaks the jaws of the Fenris Wolf with his thick shoe.

Våle is the son of Odin and *Rind*. He is a brave warrior and a good marksman. He does not wash or shave or cut his hair before he has killed Hod, Balder's slayer. Like Vidar, he survives the destruction of the world.

Høne was one of the eldest of the gods. This is how it came about that he was given to the Vaner: The Æsir had a war with the Vaner. They ravaged each other's lands, and did considerable damage. But when they grew tired of this, they summoned a council and made peace, and exchanged hostages. The Vaner gave their finest men, *Njord* and *Frey* (his son), but the Æsir gave Høne, and said that he was well-suited to be a chieftain. He was a big man and fair to look at. Along with him the Æsir sent Mime the Wise. When Høne came to Vanaheim, the Vaner made him a chieftain at once. Mime often gave him advice. But when Høne was alone at the court and Mime was away, and they came to him with difficult matters, he always replied in the same way: "Let the others advise." Then the Vaner started thinking that the Æsir had tricked them in their exchange of men. They took Mime and chopped off his head, and sent it to the Æsir. Odin chanted incantations over it, so that it talked to him and told him many things worth knowing.

Æge is of Jotun stock. He is the god of the sea, and his name is an ancient word for sea. At first he was not friendly with the Æsir, but with his sharp glance Tor frightened him into giving a feast for them each winter in his hall. Since then, he himself journeys about on visits to the Æsir, and is well-received by them. His feasts were lively, the ale poured itself, and glittering gold was used instead of firelight.

NJORD AND FREY

Njord was not of Æsir stock. He was raised in Vanaheim, but was given to the Æsir as a hostage. From this time, he remained with them, and was counted as one of the foremost among them.

He lives at *Noatun*, the hall of ships. It lies by the sea, and swans and other sea fowl are swimming outside. Njord was married to *Skade*, the daughter of a jotun, and this is how it came about: The Æsir had slain her father, *Tjatse*, who lived up in the mountains at *Trymheim* (the realm of storms). Skade wanted to avenge the slaying, and, taking helmet, coat of mail and weapons, she rushed to Asgard. The Æsir offered to come to terms with her, and gave her permission to choose a husband from among them. But she was only allowed to see their feet, and she was to choose from them. Then she caught sight of some really pretty feet, and thinking they belonged to Balder, she chose this man. But it was Njord, not Balder, that she had chosen. Njord and Skade did not get along together very well. Skade wanted to live in her old home, Trymheim, but Njord was happiest by the sea. So then they agreed to take turns living in Trymheim and Noatun. But after Njord had been in Trymheim for nine nights, he had had more than enough of the mountains. He was downright tired of them, he said. The howling of the wolves was terrible when he compared it with the swan-song he was accustomed to. But Skade fared no better. After three nights in Noatun, she complained that she could not sleep. The shrieking of the birds and the booming of the sea kept her awake. So they parted. Skade went home to Trymheim, and here she walks on skis and hunts for animals. For this reason she is called the "Ski Goddess":

Njord rules over the course of the winds, and over the sea and fire. He should be invoked if one wants good fortune at sea, and with the catch, and he gives wealth to those who pray to him for it – both land and chattels.

Frey is Njord's son. He is handsome and powerful, and one of the most highly-esteemed of the Æsir. He dwells in Alvheim, and rules over the elves of light. He drives in a chariot which is drawn by the boar *Gyllenbuste*. It can go though the air and on the sea, and its golden bristles shine like the sun. Never is it so dark at night or in the dark regions that it does not have enough light. Dwarfs built the skip *Skibladne,* and gave it to Frey. It is the best ship that has ever been made, and so large that there is room for all the Æsir on it, with their weapons and their armor. As soon as the sails are set, it always has fair winds, and on it Frey can sail wherever he wishes, for it can go on both land and sea. And it is made of so many small pieces, and with such great skill, that he can fold it up like a cloth, and put it in his pocket.

Frey is married to Gerd, the beautiful daughter of a jotun. He loved her so much that he gave away his wonderful sword to get her, and he later comes to miss it sorely. Frey has a servant named *Skirne* (the radiant). He helped him when he was wooing Gerd, and it was he who received the sword.

Frey rules over rain and sunshine, over the yield of the earth, and over prosperity and happiness among mankind. He should be invoked for a good year and peace. He is called the "god of the crops" and the "provider of abundance". He is good and mild, and brings sorrow to no one.

THE GODDESSES

Frigg is the foremost of the goddesses. She is Odin's wife and Balder's mother. Two great sorrows are to befall her: the first that Balder dies, the other that the wolf devours Odin. Frigg knows the destiny of mankind just as well as Odin, but she does not reveal what she knows. Her home is the magnificent *Fensal*.

Freya is the most highly-esteemed goddess next to Frigg. She is also called the *Vane Goddess,* for she is descended from the Vaner, but was sent to the Æsir along with her father, Njord, and her brother, Frey. In every battle, Freya has the right to half of the fallen warriors, and she herself is allowed to choose the ones she wants. She drives in a chariot drawn by two cats, and she owns the fine *Brising necklace.* Once, Loki had stolen this necklace from her. He hid it in the sea at a place called *Singastein,* and then he turned himself into a seal to keep an eye on it there. But Heimdall also turned himself into a seal and forced Loki to give up the necklace. Freya's husband is called *Od.* But he left her and went away to foreign lands. Freya often cries tears of longing for him, and her tears are of pure gold. She can be invoked if one wishes to win the love of someone else.

Vår is the goddess of fidelity. She hears the promises which men and women make to one another, and takes revenge on the one who breaks the promise.

Gevjon is a virgin, and to her comes everyone who dies as a virgin. She knows the destiny of mankind just as well as Odin and Frigg. It is told that she was with Odin and his following, when he once came to *Odinsøy* (Odense) on Fyn. Then he sent

her north over the sound, and she came to King Gylve in Svitjod (Sweden). She asked him for all the land she could plough in a day, and this she was granted. Then she rushed to Jotunheim, and there she had four sons with a jotun. These she changed into oxen. She hitched them to the plough and ploughed loose all the land that was where Lake Milar is now. This land she dragged out into the Baltic, and it became what is now called *Zealand*. There she settled down, and was wedded to *Skjold,* one of Odin's sons.

Idun is the wife of *Brage.* She keeps hidden in a box the apples which the gods bite when they start growing old. Thus they are afraid to lose Idun, and once, when she was carried off by Tjatse, a jotun, they were quite badly off.

Nanna was Balder's wife. She loved him so much that her heart broke from grief, when he was killed and placed upon the pyre.

LOKI AND HIS STOCK

Loki is the son of *Fårbaute,* a jotun, but became Odin's foster brother, and was taken up among the Æsir as one of them. He is fair and handsome, but is malicious and not to be trusted. He is wilier than anyone else, and full of all kinds of cunning devices. He often brings the gods into great difficulties, and it happens, at times, that he must help them out again – but he is and remains their enemy and the secret friend of the jotuns. His wife is called *Sigyn,* and their sons are *Vale* and *Nare.*

But Loki has several other children too. *Angerboda* is the name of a giantess who lived in Jotunheim. By her Loki had three children: *The Fenris Wolf, The Serpent of Midgard,* and *Hel,* a loathsome woman. But the gods knew that these three had been born up in Jotunheim, and from prophesies they knew that they would bring great misfortune upon them. And so Odin sent the gods to take the children, and bring them to Asgard. The Æsir did not want to kill them, for the course of destiny must not be broken, and Asgard was a holy sanctuary which must not be violated. But the Father of the Universe wanted to get rid of them by others means.

He cast the Serpent out in the sea which lies around the land, and there it grew so that it lies in the middle of the sea around the earth, and bites itself in its tail. This is why it is called the *Serpent of Midgard.*

The Father of the Universe cast Hel down in Nivlheim, and set her to rule there. She is to receive everyone who comes there, and this is everyone who dies of illness or old age. Her residence

29

is often called *Hel-vite* (Hel's place of punishment). The road to it is called *Helveg*. This road leads north, down through deep, dark valleys, and over the foaming river *Gjoll,* Across it lies the *Gjallar Bridge* which is covered with gold. Around her home is a high fence, and the great gate is called Hel's Gate. When ghosts were abroad, it was said that Hel's Gate stood open, for then they could slip out. Hel's hall is revolting: her dish is called "Hunger", her knife "Starvation", the threshold "Accident", the bed "Sick-bed", and the bed-curtain "Disaster". Hel, herself, is blue-black on one side, and of an ordinary hue on the other. Thus she is easy to recognise, and her face is grim and hideous. Her enormous dog is called *Garm*. Its breast and jaws are bloodied, and it howls terrifyingly outside of Gnipaheller, where it stands tied. There it must stand until Ragnarok, but then it will come loose. When that time is nigh, Hel's sooty-brown rooster will also crow.

The Æsir reared the wolf at home, but none save Ty was brave enough to go to him and feed him. But when the gods saw how much he grew each day, and they understood that he would come to do them great harm, they decided to bind him. They made a strong chain and carried it to the wolf. They said he was to try his strength on it. This seemed easy to the wolf, and he let them do as they liked and bind him. But the first time he lunged, the chain broke. Then the gods made a chain that was twice as strong, and told the wolf to try this one. He would be famous for his strength, they said, if a chain wich had been so strongly forged could not hold him. The wolf thought that, in all likelihood, this chain was unusually strong, but his strength had also grown since he had broken the first. And then he thought that he had to risk something, if he were to be famous. So he permitted himself to be bound by this chain. When the Æsir had finished binding him, the wolf shook himself, lunged and broke the chain so the pieces were scattered far and wide. After this the Æsir were afraid that they would not be able to bind the wolf. Then the Almighty

30

Father sent Skirne, Frey's servant, down to the realm of the elves
of darkness, to some dwarfs, and had them make a chain. It was
forged of the sound of a cat's footsteps, the beard of a woman,
the roots of the mountain, the sinews of the bear, the breath of
the fish, and the spit of the bird. That is why these things are no
more. The chain was as smooth and as soft to the touch as a silken
band, but it was solid and strong. When the chain came to the
Æsir, they thanked the messenger for an errand well done. Then
they rushed out to the isle of *Lyngve* in the lake called *Åm-
svartne*. They persuaded the wolf to come with them, and showed
him the chain and asked him to break it. It was, of course, a little
stronger than it looked, they said, and one of them handed the
end to another, and they tried to break it with their hands. This
they could not do. But the wolf could surely break it, they said.
Then the wolf replied, "It looks to me as if there would be little
honor in my breaking such a thin band. And if this is done by
trickery and treachery, that band will not come upon my feet."

But the Æsir said that he could surely break so thin a silken band, he, who had broken thick iron chains before. "And if you can't do it," they said, "you needn't be afraid of us gods. We shall release you all right." The wolf said, "I have little desire to have this band placed upon me, but I shall allow it if one of you places his hand in my mouth as a guarantee that this is done without treachery." The Æsir stood there looking at one another, and no one wanted to risk his hand. Then Ty held out his hand, and put it in the wolf's mouth. When the wolf lunged this time, the chain tightened, and the harder he struggled the stronger it became. Then all the Æsir laughed save Ty. He had lost his hand. When the Æsir saw that the wolf was bound, they took the end of the chain and drove it through a great slab. Then they pounded the slab down in the ground, and placed a huge stone over it. The wolf snapped viciously, and lunged back and forth wanting to bite them. But they stuck a sword in his mouth, with the hilt in his lower jaw and the tip in the upper jaw. He howls hideously, and froth pours from his jaws until there is a whole river of it. Thus the Fenris Wolf remains bound until Ragnarok.

Loki is the father – or, more correctly, the mother – of yet another child, Sleipne, Odin's horse. This is how it came about: When the gods had created Midgard, a jotun smith came to them. He offered to build, in a year and a half, a castle which would be safe against the frost giants. But he demanded Freya, and the sun and the moon as payment. The Æsir conferred about this, and agreed to give him the payment he demanded. But then the castle had to be finished in one winter, and he was not allowed to have help from anyone. If any of the work was unfinished by the first day of summer, he would not receive the payment. Nonetheless, the jotun asked to be allowed to have his stallion to help him, and Loki strongly advised that he be allowed to do so.

The jotun started the work on the first day of winter. During the nights he drove forth the stones with the help of his stallion, and the Æsir marvelled at the size of the stones it could drag.

When it was getting on towards spring, the jotun worked hard, and when only three days were left until the first day of summer, the castle was ready save for the gate. The Æsir were not too happy about this, for they could never give away Freya, and the sun and the moon. They held council and asked one another who was most to blame for their being in such a bad predicament, and it occurred to them that it was Loki. He had advised them to let the jotun use his stallion to help him. When they confronted Loki with this, he became frightened, and vowed to fix it so that the jotun should lose his payment – he, Loki, would surely find a way of doing this.

The same evening, when the jotun drove out to get stones with his stallion, a mare sprang out of the forest. It neighed and rushed about so that the stallion worked itself loose, and sprang after it into the forest, and the jotun rushed after them to try to catch the stallion. They ran about in the forest the whole night, and the work had to rest. Nor did they work on the following day as they had done before. When the jotun now saw that he would not be able to finish the job in the right time, his jotun rage descended upon him. The Æsir shouted for Tor, and Tor came at once. Then Mjølne the hammer flew through the air and crushed the jotun's skull.

Later the mare gave birth to a grey foal with eigth legs. This was Sleipne, but the mare was none other than Loki, himself.

TJATSE AND IDUN

Two of the Æsir – Odin and Höne – set out from home one day with Loki. They journeyed over mountains and through desolate wastes, and food was scarce. But at last they came down to a valley where they saw a herd of fine oxen. They killed one, made up a fire, and started to roast the meat. After a while, when they thought it was done, they looked at it, but it was still raw. Then they waited even longer, but when they looked at it again, the meat was not cooked this time either. They started talking about this, and wondered what was causing it. Then they heard a voice up in the oak tree under which they were sitting, and when they looked up they caught sight of an eagle, and he was not so small either. The eagle said that the meat would not cook unless he willed it to cook. "But if you'll let me eat my fill of the oxen, then it'll soon be done," he said.

This the Æsir promised. At once the eagle dropped down from the tree, and pounced upon both thighs and shoulders and was going to eat. But then Loki became furious when he saw him taking the best part of the meat, and seizing a great staff, he swung at the eagle with all his might. At the same moment the eagle flew up in the air. And now the staff stuck fast to him. Loki's hands were unable to release their hold at the other end, and so away they went. The eagle flew so low that Loki's feet were dragged over cliffs and tree tops, and he thought his arms would be torn from their sockets. He shouted and begged the eagle for mercy. But the eagle replied that Loki would never come free again unless he vowed to lure Idun out of Asgard with her apples. Loki promised, and then he was set free, and he went back to his companions. But he said nothing about his vow, and no more is told of their journey until they came home.

When the appointed time had come, Loki lured Idun out of Asgard to a forest by telling her that he had found some apples there which she would certainly like. He bade her take along her own apples so as to compare them. Then the jotun Tjatse came in the guise of an eagle, and, taking Idun, flew off with her to his hall Trymheim, where he kept her for a long time.

The Æsir were badly off when Idun and her apples were gone. They suddenly turned grey and old, and could not become young again. Then they held council, and started questioning one another as to where Idun had last been seen. It was not long before it came out that she had last been seen leaving Asgard with Loki. Then Loki was brought before the council. The Æsir threatened him with torture and death, and he became frightened, and promised to look for Idun in Jotunheim if Freya would lend him her falcon guise. This he got, and putting it on, Loki flew north to Jotunheim.

One day he came to Trymheim. Tjatse, himself, was at sea fishing, and Idun was home alone. Loki turned her into a tiny nut, and, taking it in his claws, set out for home the fastest he could. When Tjatse came home and found Idun was gone, he put on his eagle guise and set out after Loki, and it was not long before he started to overtake him.

When the Æsir caught sight of the falcon flying with the eagle in pursuit, they went outside Asgard's wall and gathered together a great pile of wooden chips. The falcon flew in over the wall, and dropped down behind it like an arrow. The Æsir bided their time, and set fire to the dry chips just as the eagle was about to fly over the wall after the falcon. He was unable to stop. His feathers took fire and he could no longer fly. The Æsir were there waiting, and Tjatse was slain just inside the gates of Asgard.

News of this slaying spread far and wide, for Tjatse was one of the mightiest and richest of the jotuns. Skade, Tjatse's daughter, took her helmet and coat of mail, and rushed to Asgard to avenge her father. But of this, and how she got Njord for her husband, we have heard before.

TOR FETCHES HIS HAMMER

Once, Tor lay sleeping, and when he woke up he discovered that his hammer was gone. His rage knew no bounds, and shaking his beard, tearing his hair and waving his arms wildly, he woke up Loki. "Listen, Loki!" he said. "What I'm going to tell you now is something that no one else knows, neither on earth nor in heaven: someone has stolen my hammer!"

Then they went to Freya. "Freya, will you lend me your plumage?" asked Tor, following Loki's advice. "Then I might be able to find my hammer again."

"Yes, I'd gladly give it to you even if it were of gold," replied Freya. "You would get it if it were forged of silver."

Loki put on the plumage, and then he flew until he was out of Asgard and over in Jotunheim. There sat Trym, the king of the giants, on a hill. He was braiding golden leashes for his dogs, and clipping the manes of his horses. "How are the Æsir getting along? And how are the elves getting along?" asked Trym. "Why have you come to Jotunheim alone?"

"The Æsir are badly off and the elves are badly off," replied Loki. "Are you the one who has hidden Tor's hammer?"

"Yes," said Trym. "I've hidden it 24 leagues down in the ground, and no one can fetch it up again unless he brings Freya to me for my wife."

Then Loki flew back to Asgard, and Tor met him out in the courtyard. "Has your luck been equal to your toil?" he asked. "Tell the long tidings from the air. Often the one who is seated forgets what he has to say, and the one who is lying down tells lies flippantly."

"Yes, my luck has been equal to my toil," replied Loki. "Trym the king of the frost giants, has your hammer. But the one who wants to fetch it back must bring Freya to him for his wife."

Then they went in and found Freya, and Tor said to her, "Gird the bridal linen about you Freya. Now the two of us are going to drive to Jotunheim."

But when Freya heard this, she was so furious that she fumed, and the hall shook, and the Brising necklace broke and fell from around her neck. "People would call me 'man-hungry'", she said, "if I rode with you to Jotunheim."

The Æsir held council, and the goddesses consulted one another.

The mighty gods pondered greatly over how they were to get the hammer back. Then Heimdall said, "Let us gird the bridal linen about Tor. He shall wear the Brising necklace too. Let the keys dangle from his belt, and let women's clothing fall about his knees. We will adorn his breast with broad stones, and put his hair up nicely in a knot." But then Tor said, "The Æsir will call me a weakling if I gird the bridal linen about me."

"Hush now, Tor," said Loki, "and do not talk like that! If you don't fetch your hammer, the jotuns will soon be reigning in Asgard!" So they girded the bridal linen about Tor, and fixed him the way Heimdall had said. When they had finished, Loki said, "Take me along. I shall be your maidservant. The two of us will drive to Jotunheim." The rams were brought home from the pasture, and hitched to the front of the chariot. Then they set out with a vengeance. Mountains cracked and fields stood aflame wherever they sprang. Now Odin's son was driving to Jotunheim.

When Trym heard them coming he said, "Up now, jotuns, scatter straw in the hall. Now they are bringing Freya, the daughter of Njord from Noatun, to me as a bride. Here at the manor are cows with golden horns and black oxen. I have gold in piles and costly jewels. Only Freya do I still lack."

Soon evening came, and the food was borne forth to the table for the jotuns. Tor ate one ox, eight salmon, and all the delicacies that had been set aside for the women, and he drank three barrels of mead.

Then Trym said, "Have you ever seen a bride take bigger bites? Never have I seen a bride eat more greedily, nor any maiden drink more mead." But the wily servant was ready with an answer: "Freya hasn't eaten for eight days, so great was her desire to come to Jotunheim." Trym lifted the veil. He wanted to kiss the bride. But he flew back the length of the hall, "Why are Freya's eyes so bright? It's as though fire is flashing from them." Loki had an answer ready this time too: "Freya hasn't slept for eight nights, such was her longing to come to Jotunheim."

Now the wretched jotun-sister came in to ask for a gift from the bride. "Before you can win my friendship, you must give me burnished rings," she said. Then Trym said, "Bring the hammer, place Mjölne in the lap of the bride, wed us together in the name of the goddess Vår." Tor laughed in his beard when he felt the handle of the hammer in his hands. First he slew Trym, the king of the frost giants, and then all of his stock. He killed the old jotun-sister, too — the one who had asked for a gift from the bride.

This is how Tor got back his hammer.

TOR AND UTGARD-LOKI

One day Tor set out with his rams and his chariot, and Loki was with him. Towards evening they came to a farm, and the farmer put them up for the night. In the evening Tor took the rams and slaughtered them. They were flayed and put in the kettle, and when they were cooked, Tor and Loki sat down to supper. The farmer's son was called *Tjalve,* and the daughter *Roskva.* Tor spread the goatskins between the door and the fire, and said that the farmer and his household were to throw the bones over on the skins. But Tjalve was busy with the thighbone of one of the rams, he split it with his knife and broke it, for he wanted to get hold of the marrow.

Then Tor spent the night there, and early the next morning he got up and put on his clothes. He took the hammer, swung it and made the goatskins whole with it. Then the rams stood up, but one was lame in one of its hind legs. Tor noticed this, and said that the farmer or one of his people had not been careful with the ram's bone the night before, for he could tell that the thighbone was broken. Everyone can imagine how frightened the farmer was now, when he saw Tor's eyebrows drawing down over his eyes, and what he saw of his eyes was enough to make him think he would faint. Tor seized the handle of the hammer so his knuckles whitened. But the farmer and his household did what could be expected: they shrieked terribly and pleaded for mercy, and offered Tor everything they owned to make good. When he saw how frightened they were, his anger left him, and he took the children, Tjalve and Roskva, as compensation from the farmer. They became servants, and they have followed him constantly ever since.

Tor left the rams behind, and set out on the journey east to Jotunheim. He came to the sea, and embarked upon it. When he came to land, he went upwards, and Loki and Tjalve and Roskva went with him. When they had gone a little while, they came to a great forest, and they walked in it the whole day until it started growing dark. Tjalve was quite fleet-footed, and he carried Tor's bag of provisions. When it was dark, they started looking around for a shelter for the night. They found a very large house, too. In one end there was a doorway just as wide as the house itself. There they lay down to sleep. But in the middle of the night there was a great earthquake, the ground trembled beneath them and the house shook. Then Tor got up and shouted to his companions. They groped their way about and came to a side room in the middle of the house. There Tor sat down in the doorway. The others were farther inside. They were all quite frightened, and Tor held his hammer in his hand and thought to protect himself. They heard a loud droning.

When morning came, Tor went out and caught sight of a man who was lying in the forest a short distance away, and he was no little fellow! He lay sleeping, and was snoring loudly. Then Tor thought he knew what the droning had been that they heard during the night. He girded the strength-giving belt about himself, and his Æsir strength grew. But at the same moment, the man awoke and suddenly stood up, and it is said that for once Tor was afraid to strike. He asked the man his name. He called himself *Skryme*. "But I don't have to ask your name," he said, "for I can see that you are Tor. But what have you done with my glove?" And Skryme bent down and picked up the glove. Then Tor saw that this was what he had taken to be a house during the night, and the side room had been the thumb of the glove.

Skryme asked if Tor would have him as a travelling companion, and to this he said yes. Then Skryme opened his sack of food and sat down to eat breakfast, and Tor and his companions sat down in another spot. Skryme then asked if they shouldn't put their food together, and to this Tor agreed. Then Skryme tied all the food in one sack, and put it on his back. He went ahead of them the whole day, and took rather long strides, and not until late at night did he find shelter for them under a great oak. Then he told Tor that he wanted to go to sleep. "But you take the sack of food and have something to eat," he added.

Soon Skryme was asleep, and snoring so it thundered. Tor took the sack of food and wanted to open it. But not one knot was he able to untie, and not one strap was he able to make looser than before. Now, when he saw that all his struggles were to no avail, he became angry, and taking Mjölne with both hands, he strode over to where Skryme lay. He struck him on the head. But Skryme woke up and asked if a leaf had fallen on his head, and whether they had got something to eat and were ready to go to sleep. Tor said they were just going to, and then they went over to another oak and lay down. But they did not feel safe where they were lying. In the middle of the night, Tor heard that Skryme was fast asleep, and snoring so the forest rumbled. Then he got up and went over to him, swung the hammer quickly and hard, and hit him right in the middle of his crown. He felt the head of the hammer sink down deep into the head. But Skryme woke up and asked what was going on. "Was that an acorn that fell on my head?" he asked. "How are you getting on, Tor?" Tor replied that he had just awakened, and then hurried back. It was now the middle of the night, he said, and still time left for sleeping.

Now Tor thought that if he had an opportunity of striking at Skryme a third time, the jotun would not see the light of day any more. So he lay down, and kept watch to see whether Skryme should fall asleep again. Shortly before daybreak he heard that Skryme was asleep. Then he got up, sprang over to him, swung his hammer with all his might, and let fly at him in the temple which was turned up. The hammer sank in right up to the handle, but Skryme sat up, stroked his cheek and said, "I wonder if there's a bird sitting in the tree above me? It seemed to me when I awoke that some twigs fell on my head. Are you awake, Tor? It's probably time to get up and get dressed. Now you haven't far to go to the castle of Utgard. I've heard you whispering among yourselves that I'm not small of stature, but you'll see bigger fellows when you come to Utgard. Now I'll give you some good advice: Don't be too swell-headed! Utgard-Loki's men won't stand bragging from such little fellows as you. Otherwise you ought to turn back, and I think this would be the best thing for you. But if you absolutely must go on, then you have to head east. I'm going north to those mountains you see over there." Skryme took the sack of provisions and slung it on his back. Then he left and went straight into the forest, and no one has heard that Tor and his companions wished him Godspeed.

Tor and his companions kept going until noon. Then they saw a castle that stood on a plain, and the castle was so high that they had to bend over backwards if they wanted to see the top. They went over to it, but the gate to the castle was closed, and for all Tor tried he could not get it open. But they wanted to enter the castle, and so they crept between the bars and went in that way. They saw a great hall and walked towards it. The door stood open and they went in. Here sat many men on two benches, and most of them were excessively huge. Then they came forth to the king, Utgard-Loki, and greeted him. But he took his time before he looked at them, sneered contemptuously and said, "Nay, is that little fellow Tor the Charioteer? But maybe you're bigger than you look! What sports do you and your companions think you're ready for? For no one can remain here with us without having some art or skill in which he excels over and above most people."

Loki, who had come last, now said, "I have a sport that I'm ready to try at once. There's no one in here who can eat his food

faster than I can." Then Utgard-Loki replied, "Well, that's a
sport if you manage it, and we'll try it at once." He shouted down
along the bench for someone called *Loge* to come forth, and have
an eating-match with Loki. Then a trough filled with meat was
carried in and placed on the floor. Loki sat at one end and Loge
at the other. Both ate the fastest they had learned, and they met in
the middle of the trough. Then Loki had eaten all the meat off
the bones, but Loge had eaten all the meat, and the bones and the
trough as well, and everyone agreed that Loki had lost the match.

Then Utgard-Loki asked what Tjalve could do, and he said
that he wanted to try to have a foot-race with whoever Utgard-
Loki picked out. Utgard-Loki said that this was a good sport,
but he had to be fleet of foot in order to manage it, but this they
would soon see. He stood up and went out on the flat plain.
Here he called a little boy named *Huge* over to him, and said
he was to race with Tjalve. When they had finished the first lap,
Huge was so far ahead that he had turned towards Tjalve at the
goal. Then Utgard-Loki said, "You must indeed exert yourself
harder, Tjalve, if you want to win the contest; nonetheless I
think, if the truth be told, that a swifter man has never come
here." Then they took another lap, and when Huge had come
to the goal and looked back, it was still a long bow-shot to Tjalve.
Then Utgard-Loki said, "Tjalve runs well, but I don't think he'll

win the contest, but this we'll see now when they run the third lap." When Huge came to the goal and turned this time, Tjalve was not even halfway, and now everyone said that this contest had lasted long enough.

Then Utgard-Loki asked Tor which sports he wanted to show them, since rumors had spread about his great feats. Tor said that he would prefer to have a drinking-contest with someone. Utgard-Loki said this could be arranged, and went into the hall and told his steward to bring out the great horn from which the men had to drink when they were being punished. The steward came with the horn, and put it in Tor's hands. "It is considered well drunk when someone empties this horn at one draught. Some empty it in two, but no one is such a bad drinker that he cannot empty it in three." Tor looked at the horn. It did not seem very big, but it was rather long. But Tor was quite thirsty, and started drinking in great gulps. He thought he would not have to bend over the horn again. But when he could drink no more, and looked to see how much the liquid had gone down in the horn, he thought that he could see little or no difference. "You drank well," said Utgard-Loki, "but not an excessive amount. I wouldn't have thought it, if anyone had said so, that Tor the Charioteer couldn't drink more. But now I know that you'll empty it at the second try." Tor did not reply. He put the horn to his mouth and thought that now he would take a greater draught than the first time. He drank all he could. Nonetheless, he saw that the other end of the horn didn't come up as high as he wished, and, when he took the horn from his mouth and looked down in it, he thought instead that the liquid had gone down less than before. But now the horn could be carried without spilling over. Then Utgard-Loki said, "Now, Tor, you're not sparing more for the last drink than you want to? It looks as though the most has been left for the third drink. No, you can't be counted as such a man here as with Æsir, if you can't do better for yourself in other contests than in this." Then Tor became angry, put the horn to his mouth and drank for dear life – as long as he could, but when he looked down in the horn this time, he saw that it had gone down only a little. Then he gave up.

"It's now plain to see," said Utgard-Loki, "that you can't accomplish as much as we thought. Do you want to try other contests? You see there's no use with this one." Tor replied, "Yes, I must try some others. But it would be strange if back home with the Æsir they would say that this had been poorly drunk. What kind of a contest will you offer me now?" "Our little boys," said Utgard-Loki, "engage in some trifles. They lift my cat off the ground. I wouldn't even have mentioned it to Tor the Charioteer, if I hadn't seen that you are much smaller than I'd thought." Then a grey, rather large cat sprang forth onto the floor. Tor went over to it, put his hand under its stomach, and lifted. But the cat only curved its back as Tor raised his hand. Tor stretched himself into the air as high as he could, but the cat only lifted up one foot, and Tor made no headway with this contest either. "This ended just as I had expected," said Utgard-Loki. "If anything, the cat is big and Tor is little and lowly, as compared to such big fellows as we have here." Then Tor said, "As little as you say I am, let anyone who wishes come and wrestle with me! Now I am angry!"

Utgard-Loki looked around at the benches and said, "I can't see anyone here who wouldn't think it a shame to wrestle with you. But let's see – call in Elle, my foster mother, then Tor can wrestle with her if he wants to. She has thrown men who haven't looked weaker than Tor." So an old hag came into the hall, and Utgard-Loki said that she was to wrestle with Tor. Out they jumped and it seemed that the harder Tor took hold of her, the firmer she stood. The old hag then started using tricks. They took some strong holds, and it wasn't long before Tor had to go down on one knee. Then Utgard-Loki went over to them and said that it was enough, Tor certainly didn't want to offer to wrestle with any more of his people. Now it had also grown late in the evening, and Utgard-Loki showed Tor and his companions to seats. They spent the night there, and were waited on upon in the best manner.

As soon as it started growing light, Tor and his companions got up, dressed, and made ready to journey on their way. Utgard-Loki had a table set for them, and there was no lack of food or drink. When they had eaten, they set out on the way. Utgard-Loki went out of the gate with them. When they were to part, he asked Tor what he thought of his journey. Tor replied that he could only say that he departed from there in great shame.

"I know you will say I am a poor weakling," he said, "and I don't like this at all." Then Utgard-Loki said, "Now that you have come out of the castle, I will tell you how things really are. If I am to live and reign, you shall never come inside my castle again. And one thing is certain, you never would have come in there now, had I known beforehand that you were so strong, for you were on the verge of leading us into great misfortune. I have tricked you: the first time when we met in the forest, when you were to open up the sack of provisions, I had bound it with magic yarn. That is why you were unable to get it open. Then you gave me three blows with your hammer. The first was the lightest, but it was hard enough to have killed me if it had landed. Near my hall you saw a flat mountain with three square valleys in it, one deeper than the other. Those were the marks from your hammer. I shot the mountain in between the blows, but you didn't see it. So it was, too, with the contests you tried with my men. Loki was hungry and ate greedily, but Loge was the untamed fire, and burned the trough just as fast as the meat. The Huge with whom Tjalve raced, was my memory or thought, and it wasn't to be expected that Tjalve could run as fast as that. You drank from the horn and thought it went slowly, but to tell the truth, it was so great a wonder that I hadn't thought anything like it could happen. The other end of the horn lay out in the sea, but you didn't know that. But when you come to the sea, you can see how much it has gone down. Folk now call it 'ebb tide'. Nor did I think it less of a wonder when you raised the cat, and to tell the truth, everyone was afraid when they saw it lift one of its paws off the ground. For that wasn't a cat, though you thought it was. It was the Serpent of Midgard which lies all around the land. It was barely long enough for the head and tail to touch the earth, and you lifted it so high that there was only a little distance left to heaven. It was also a great wonder, when you wrestled with Elle, that you remained standing so long and fell down on only one knee, for no one has done that, and no one will do it without Elle, or 'Old Age', winning over him. Now we shall part, and it is best for us both that you don't come here any more. The next time, too, I shall protect my castle with some trick or other."

When Tor heard this, he grabbed his hammer and swung it in the air, but when he was going to strike, Utgard-Loki was nowhere to be seen. He went back and wanted to tear down the castle, but he saw only broad and fair plains and no castle. Then he turned again, and journeyed on his way until he came home to Trudvang. But he made up his mind to go out again soon, and this time he wanted to set out against the Serpent of Midgard.

TOR FISHES FOR THE SERPENT OF MIDGARD

Tor did not stay at home long. He set out on the new journey so fast that he had neither chariot, nor rams, nor companions with him. He went off in the guise of a young man.

In the evening he came to a jotun called *Hyme,* and there he spent the night. At daybreak, Hyme got up, dressed himself and made ready to row out to sea. He wanted to go fishing. Then Tor sprang up, was ready in a flash, and asked Hyme if he could come with him. But Hyme said that he could not be of much help, as little and young as he was, "And you'll freeze if I sit as long and as far out as I usually do," he said. Tor said that Hyme could row as far from land as he wanted to, and he shouldn't be too certain which one of them would first ask to be allowed to come ashore. Tor was so mad at the jotun that he could have hit him with his hammer then and there, but he let it be, for he thought to try his strength elsewhere.

He asked the jotun what they were going to use for bait, but Hyme said that Tor would have to get his own. A short distance away, Tor saw a herd of fine oxen which Hyme owned. He went over and wrenched off the head of the biggest ox, and this he took with him. When he came down to the shore, Hyme had got the boat out, and they rowed off. Tor sat in the back of the boat, took a pair of oars, and rowed so hard that even Hyme thought it went pretty fast. After a while Hyme said that they were now at the spot where he usually fished for halibut. Tor could put up the oars, he said. But Tor said that he wanted to row much farther out, and they rowed a good bit farther. Then Hyme said

that now they had come so far that it was dangerous to row any longer because of the Serpent of Midgard. But Tor still wanted to row for a while, and this he did, and Hyme was quite ill at ease.

At last Tor pulled in the oars. He made ready a strong line, and took forth a fishhook which suited it. It was both big and strong. Then he put the head of the ox on the hook, and threw it out. And the Serpent of Midgard let itself be lured. It bit over the ox head, and the hook went into its gum. But when the Serpent felt that, it jerked so hard that both of Tor's fists smashed against the gunnels. Then Tor became angry and put on his Æsir strength. He pulled so hard that both feet went through the boat and he was standing on the sea bottom. Now he dragged the Serpent up to the gunnels, and no one has seen a more horrible sight than when Tor flashed his eyes at the Serpent, and the Serpent glared back, spouting venom. Hyme changed color. He turned pale and became frightened when he saw the Serpent, and the water pouring in and out of the boat. And at the same moment that Tor snatched up the hammer and raised it high, the jotun fumbled for the bait knife, chopped off the line against the gunnels, and the Serpent sank into the sea again. Tor hurled the hammer after it, and some say that he knocked off its head. But the truth probably is that the Serpent of Midgard still lives at the bottom of the sea. Tor swung at Hyme under the ear with his fist, so that he plunged overboard with both feet in the air. Tor, himself, waded ashore.

TOR FIGHTS WITH RUNGNE

Tor had gone east to slay trolls. Then Odin rode to Jotunheim on Sleipne, and came to the jotun *Rungne*. The jotun asked him what manner of man he was, with a golden helmet on his head, who could ride both through the air and over the sea. And what a good horse he had. Odin replied that he would wager his head that a better horse was not to be found in all Jotunheim. Rungne said that of course Odin's horse was good, but he, himself, had one that was much faster. Odin rode on his way. But Rungne had now become angry, and springing up on his horse, he set out after him. He would repay him for his boasting. Odin rode so hard that he was slighty in the lead the whole time. But Rungne was now in such a jotun rage that, before he knew what was happening, he was inside the gates of Asgard. And when he came to the door of the hall, the Æsir bade him come in to a drinking party. He accepted, and went into the hall.

Here the bowls from which Tor usually drank were set out. Rungne emptied them all as though they were nothing. When he had now become drunk, there was no end to the boasting. He was going to take Valhall, he said, and move it to Jotunheim, sink Asgard and kill all the gods save Freya and Siv, Tor's wife. He was going to take them home with him. Freya was the only one who dared pour for him, and he was going to drink up all the ale the Æsir had, he said.

The Æsir were soon tired of his boasting. They named Tor by name, and at once Tor was standing in the hall, holding his hammer in the air. He was in a terrible rage, and asked who was to blame that sly jotuns were drinking here. Who had given Rungne permission to be in Valhall, and why was Freya waiting on him as at the Æsir's feasts? Rungne did not regard Tor any too kindly, and said that Odin, himself, had invited him to a drinking party and given him sanctuary. Tor said that, before he was through, he would be anything but pleased by this hospitality. Tor would have little honor from slaying him unarmed, said Rungne. Greater courage would be needed if he would fight with him at his dwelling. "It was stupid of me", he said, "to leave my shield and whetstone at home, for if I'd had my weapons here, we would have had a trial by combat right away. But if you should kill me unarmed, you will be called a coward." Tor would by no means refuse to come and fight with Rungne, for it was the first time anyone had offered him a trial by combat.

Then Rungne rushed off, and rode as hard as he could until he came to Jotunheim. There he received much praise for his journey, and it was made known far and wide that he was to meet Tor in combat. But the jotuns knew that there was a lot at stake for them. Rungne was the strongest of them all, and if he fell, they could expect no mercy from Tor. So they made a clay man 27 leagues high and 9 leagues wide under the arms. They were unable to find a heart big enough for him until they took the heart out of a mare, but when Tor came, it turned out that even this heart was not brave enough. But Rungne had a heart of stone, and what is more it was three-sided. His head was also of stone, and so was his shield, which was big and thick. Now, while he stood waiting for Tor, he held the shield in front of him. He had his whetstone on his shoulders. He wanted to use it as a weapon. He was not at all to be trifled with as he stood there. By his side stood the clay jotun, but he was so frightened that he did not know what to do with himself.

Tor came with Tjalve to the combat. Tjalve ran ahead, and over to Rungne. "Hey, jotun!" he said. "You're holding your shield in front of you, but Tor has seen you and is coming under the ground, and now he's coming up right underneath you." Then Rungne put the shield under his feet and stood on it, and he took the whetstone in both hands. At the same moment he saw a great flash of lightning, and heard a mighty crash of thunder, and then he caught sight of Tor. He came in his Æsir strength, and rushed forward like a tempest. He swung his hammer and threw it at the jotun from afar. Rungne raised the whetstone and threw it. It met the hammer in the air and broke into many bits. Some fell down to the ground, and from these come all whetstones. Others flew into Tor's head, and he fell as far as he was tall. But the hammer hit Rungne right in the middle of his forehead, smashing his skull to bits. He fell over Tor with his foot on his neck. In the meantime, Tjalve had fought with the clay jotun, and had won an easy victory over him. Now he went over to Tor and wanted to lift the jotun foot off him, but he was unable to budge it. When the Æsir heard that Tor had fallen, they all came and tried to move the foot away, but it was of no use. But then Tor's son, *Magne,* came. He was then three winters old. He threw the foot off Tor right away. "It was a pity for my father," he said, "that I came so late. I would have killed that jotun with my bare fists, had I but met him." Then Tor got up and received his son well. "He will amount to something great in time," he said, "and now I want to give you Rungne's horse," he added. Then Odin said that Tor had done wrong to give the horse away to the son of a jotun woman and not to his own father.

Now Tor rushed home to Trudvang. The pieces of whetstone sat fast in his head, and so he went to a seeress called *Groa.* She chanted her incantations over Tor, and the whetstone loosened. When Tor felt this, he thought that he was about to be rid of the pieces of stone, and so he wanted to reward Groa for her efforts, and make her happy. He told her that he had been north, and waded over Elivågar. Then he had carried her husband in a basket on his back from Jotunheim. As proof that this was true, he mentioned that one of his toes stuck out of the basket, and had frozen so stiff that Tor had broken it off, and thrown it up to the heavens and made a star of it. Now it would not be long, he said, before her husband came home. But when Groa heard this, she became so happy that she forgot all her incantations. And so the pieces of whetstone did not become any looser, and they are still in Tor's skull.

TOR AND GEIRRØD THE JOTUN

Once Loki put on Frigg's falcon guise, and took a flight in it for fun. Then he wanted to see how things looked at the manor of *Geirröd* the jotun, and so there he flew.

He alighted in an opening, and looked into the great hall. Geirröd caught sight of the bird, and ordered one of his men to catch it and bring it to him. But it was not easy for the man to climb up the wall, for it was quite high. Loki thought it was fun to watch him toil so to catch hold of him, and so he remained sitting where he was. There would always be time enough to fly away once the man had come up, he thought. But when he wanted to kick out and fly, his feet sat fast, and Loki was captured and taken to the jotun.

When Geirröd looked him in the eyes, he understood that this was no bird that he had before him, but a man who had taken on the guise of a bird. Geirröd spoke to him, but Loki did not reply. Then the jotun locked him in a chest, and let him starve there for three months. At last Geirröd took him up and spoke to him, and now Loki told who he was. In order to save his life, he swore that he would make it come to pass that Tor came to Geirröd without his hammer, or his strength-giving belt and gloves. Then Loki was allowed to go home again.

We did not know what Loki did, but it came about that Tor set out, and both Loki and Tjalve were with him. On the way, Tor visited the jotun woman Grid, mother of Vidar the god. She told him that Geirröd was a tremendously crafty jotun, who was troublesome to have dealings with. Because of this, she lent Tor a strength-giving belt, a pair of iron gloves and her staff. Then Tor rushed on and came to a great river called *Vimur*. This he had to cross. He put on the belt, and supported himself against the current with the staff. Loki clung fast to his belt, and Tjalve hung to the straps of his shield. When Tor had come out in the middle of the river, it started rising so fast that it went over his shoulders. Then he chanted:

"Rise not, Vimur,
For I have thought to wade
Forth to the jotun manor.

Know that if you grow,
Then my Æsir strength will grow too
As high as heaven."

Then he caught sight of Geirröd's daughter *Gjalp*. She was standing up in a gulley, straddling the river, and it was she who was making the river rise. Then he took a huge stone and threw it at her.

"The river should be dammed at its source," he said. The stone landet where it should, and the current carried him so close to land that he caught hold of a rowan tree. He pulled himself up in it, and strode ashore.

When Tor came to Geirröd, he and his companions were given shelter in a goat house. There was only a single stool there, and Tor sat down on it. But after a while he felt the stool rising up to the ceiling. Then he thrust Grid's staff up against the rafters, and made himself heavy on the stool. At once there was a great cracking and shrieking underneath it. Geirröd's daughters, Gjalp and *Greip*, had been lying under the stool, and now he had broken their backs.

Now Geirröd had Tor summoned into the hall in order to test his strength. Great fires were burning down the middle of the hall, and when Tor came towards Geirröd, the jotun took a glowing bolt of iron with a pair of tongs, and threw it at him. Tor caught it with the iron gloves, and lifted it in the air, but Geirröd sprang behind a pillar and hid himself. Then Tor flung the bolt with such force that it went through the pillar, through Geirröd, through the wall and right down into the ground.

BALDERS DEATH

The origin of the portentous events which shall be related here, was that Balder the Good had been having bad dreams that bode evil for his life. He told his dreams to the Æsir, and they assembled at the council and deliberated on what to do.

Odin got up and saddled Sleipne. Then he rode straight to Nivlheim. As he approached the realm of Hel, her dog came running, with its bloodied breast, and barked at him. But Odin was not to be stopped. He rushed on so the roads of Hel boomed beneath him, until he came forth to Hel's lofty hall. There he rode at once to a spot east of the door. He knew that a *Volve* (or prophetess) lay buried there, and he wanted to speak with her. Odin chanted incantations over her, and at last she had to climb up out of the grave. She spoke with the voice of a spectre: "Who is it who forces me to go such a hard way? The snow covered me, the rain beat me, I am wet through by dew. I have already been dead for a long time."

"I am called Veg-tam," (the path-finder) said Odin, "and I am the son of Val-tam (the one accustomed to battle). Tell me now, for whom is the hall decked here in Helheim?"

"For Balder the mead, that noble drink, is ready brewed," replied the Volve, "and the gods are now in great peril. I was forced to speak. Now I must keep counsel."

"Nay, do not keep counsel, Volve," said Odin. "I wish to know more: Who will be the bane of Balder, Odin's son?" Then the Volve replied, "Hod shall bring the noble hero here, he shall be Balder's bane. But now I must keep councel."

"Do not keep counsel, Volve," said Odin. "I wish to know more: Who will punish Hod for this crime? Who will place Balder's slayer upon the pyre?"

The Volve replied: "Rind will give birth to *Våle*. One night old, he kills Balder's slayer. He does not wash his hand nor comb his hair before he carries him upon the pyre. I was forced to speak. Now I must keep counsel."

"Tell me just one thing more," said Odin. "What maidens are those who weep such heavy tears?"

Then the Volve said, "You are not Veg-tam, but Odin!"

"And you are no Volve," said Odin, "but the mother of three giants!"

"Ride home now, Odin," said the Volve, "and do not come back here before Loki is loose, and the destruction of the world is at hand."

When the mighty gods were gathered at the council, they decided to ask everything in the world for mercy for Balder against all that was evil. Frigg made all things swear an oath that they would spare Balder – fire and water, iron and all kinds of ores, stones and earth, trees and sicknesses, animals and birds, serpents and snakes. When this was done, the gods felt safe, and they even amused themselves by having Balder stand before them, while some shot at him, others swung at him, and still others threw stones at him. But no matter what they did, nothing would harm him in the least. But Loki, who stood looking on, did not like this at all. He turned himself into an old woman, and went to Frigg in Fensal. Frigg asked if the old woman knew what the Æsir were doing. She said they were all shooting at Balder, but nothing harmed him. "Neither weapons nor trees will do Balder any harm," said Frigg, "for I have bound them all by oath."

Then the old woman asked, "Is it really true that everything has vowed to protect Balder?"

"To be sure, there is a tiny twig that grows west of Valhall," said Frigg. "It is called 'mistletoe', but I thought it too young to take any oath." When Loki heard this, he went away, pulled up the mistletoe, and went to the council with it. Hod stood outermost in the ring of men, for he was blind. Loki went over to him and asked, "Why aren't you shooting at Balder?" "I cannot see where he is standing," said Hod, "and I have no weapon."

"You must do as the others, and pay Balder the same homage as they do," said Loki. "Now I will show you where he is standing. Take this twig and shoot at him." Hod took the mistletoe and shot at Balder the way Loki showed him. The shot went through Balder, and he fell dead to the ground. This is the greatest calamity that has ever befallen gods and mortals.

When Balder fell, the Æsir lost their power of speech, and no one could lift a hand to help him. Each one looked at the other, and they were all equally angry at the one who was to blame for the crime. But no one could avenge the slaying, for the spot was sanctified. When they tried to talk, they were moved to tears, and no one could interpret his grief in words to the others. Odin took the accident the hardest, for he best understood how great a loss the Æsir suffered from Balder's death. When the gods came to their senses again, Frigg asked which of them wanted to win all her favor and love by riding to Hel and trying to talk with Balder, and offering Hel a ransom so she would permit Balder to come

home again to Asgard. Hermod the Fleet, Odin's son, took the quest upon himself. Sleipne was led forth, and Hermod mounted the horse and rushed away.

The Æsir took Balder's body and carried it to the sea. His great ship had been drawn up on land. Now the gods wanted to shove it out on the water and build Balder's funeral pyre upon it, but they could not budge it from the spot. Then they sent word to Jotunheim for a giantess called *Hyrrokkin* (she who is shriveled by fire), and she came riding on a wolf with venomous snakes for reins. She sprang off, and Odin set four strong men to watch the wolf, but they were unable to hold it before they had thrown it to the ground. The giantess went to the bow of the ship and pushed it out with one shove, and with such speed that sparks flashed from the skids, and the whole earth trembled. Then Tor became angry, and seizing his hammer, would have crushed her head had not all the gods begged him to spare her. After that, Balder was carried out onto the ship, and when Nanna, his wife, saw this, she died of grief, and she too was placed upon the pyre. It was lighted, and Tor stood beside it and consecrated it with Mjølne. A dwarf was running in front of his feet. Tor kicked him up into the flames, and he burned along with it.

Many kinds of beings came to Balder's funeral. Odin was there, and with him came Frigg, and the Valkyries and his ravens. Frey drove in his chariot drawn by the boar Gyllenbuste. Heimdall rode on Gulltopp, and Freya came driving with her cats. Great crowds of frost giants and mountain giants were there too. Odin put the ring Draupne in the fire. Finally they led Balder's horse, in full trappings, out onto the pyre.

Concerning Hermod, it is related that he rode for nine nights through dark and deep valleys, and he saw nothing until he came to the river Gjoll, and rode over the Gjallar Bridge. It is made of shining gold. The maiden who stands guard at the bridge asked him his name and stock, and said that on the previous day five flocks of dead men had ridden over the bridge, "but the bridge

thunders as much under you alone as it did under all of them. Nor
have you the hue of the dead either. So why do you ride here on
the road to Hel?" "I am riding to Hel to look for Balder," replied
Hermod. "Have you seen anything of him on the road?"

It was true enough that Balder had ridden over the Gjallar
Bridge, she said, "and down to the north lies the road to Hel."
So Hermod rode on until he came to the gates of Hel. There he
dismounted and tightened the saddle girths, seated himself again,
and touched the horse with his spurs. Then it sprang so high over
the gates that it did not come near them. Hermod rode over to the
hall, dismounted and went in. There he saw Balder, his brother,
seated on the throne. Hermod spent the night there.

In the morning he asked Hel if Balder could be allowed to ride
home with him. He told her how the Æsir were crying and
mourning over him. But Hel said that she wanted to find out
whether Balder really was as highly esteemed as it was said. "If
everything in the world," she said, "living and dead, cries for
him, then he shall journey back to the Æsir. But if there is anyone
who will not cry, he shall remain with me."

Then Hermod stood up, and Balder went out of the hall with
him. Now he took off the ring Draupne, and sent it back to Odin
as a keepsake. Nanna sent a cloth to Frigg, and several other gifts.
Then Hermod rode off. He came back to Asgard, and there he
told everything he had seen and heard.

The Æsir now sent messengers out over the whole world, and
they were to ask all things to cry Balder out of Hel. And this they
all did: mortals and animals, earth, stones and trees, and all met-
als – the way we see these things cry when they come in from the

cold to warmth. But, when the messengers had carried out their errand in the best possible way, and were on their way home, they came to a cave, and here they found a troll hag. She called herself *Tokk*. They also asked her to cry Balder out of Hel. But she said:

> *"Tokk will cry*
> *dry tears*
> *over Balder's funeral pyre.*
> *Alive or dead*
> *he gave me little.*
> *Let Hel keep what she has!"*

But there are many who say that this troll hag was Loki.

LOKI IS BOUND

The gods hated Loki. First of all, he was responsible for Balder's death, and then it was his fault that Balder could not come back from Hel.

Therefore Loki ran away, and hid on a mountain. Here he built a house for himself with four doors so he could sit inside and look out on all sides. But during the day he often changed himself into a salmon, and then he stayed in a waterfall. He pondered greatly over what kind of implement the Æsir would probably think up in order to get hold of him here in the falls.

One day, as he was sitting in his house, he took flax-yarn and bound meshes of it, the way mortals have since made fishing nets. In front of him a fire was burning. Then he saw that the Æsir were not far from his house, for Odin had seen where he was from Lidskjalv. At once Loki threw the net onto the fire, and he, himself, jumped up and hurried out into the river.

The Æsir came up to the house, and Kvase the Wise went in first. He went over to the fire, and there he saw the ashes from the net that had burned there. He understood at once that it must be an implement for catching fish, and he told this to the Æsir. They sat down at once, and made a net the way they saw that Loki had done it.

When it was finished, the Æsir went down to the river and threw the net out into the falls. Tor held onto one end, and all the Æsir held onto the other, and then they dragged the net downstream. Loki swam ahead of the net, and lay down between two stones. Thus the net went over him, but they felt that something

alive had barely touched it. They went up to the falls and threw
out the net the second time, but now they had fastened something
heavy to it so that no fish could go under it. This time, too, Loki
swam ahead of the net. But when he saw that it was not far to the
sea, he sprang over the net, and rushed back to the falls again.
Now the Æsir had seen him. They went up to the falls once again.
This time they divided themselves into two groups, one group
pulling on each end, but Tor waded out to the middle of the river.
Thus they dragged the net downstream towards the sea. Now Loki
had to do one of two things: either he must swim out to sea
at the risk of his life, or else he had to jump over the net again.
He chose the latter, and jumped over it as fast as he could. But,
at the same moment, Tor grabbed at him and caught hold of him.
But the fish slipped in his hand so that Tor was unable to grasp
it tightly before his hand was back by the tail, and this is why the
salmon's back is so narrow.

70

Loki had now been caught in a place which was not a sanctuary, and so he could expect no mercy. The Æsir took him to a cave. There they took three pointed rocks, stood them on end and bored holes through them. Then they seized Loki's two sons, Vale and Nare. They turned Vale into a wolf, and he tore his brother to pieces at once. The Æsir took his guts, and with them they bound Loki over the sharp stones so that one was under his shoulders, the other under his loins, and the third under his knees. The bonds turned to iron. Skade took a venomous serpent and fastened it above him so the venom could drip down into his face. But Sigyn, Loki's wife, stands by him and holds a vessel under the dripping venom. Each time the vessel is full, she goes out and throws the venom away. But then venom drips onto Loki's face, and he writhes so hard that the whole earth trembles. This is what people call 'earthquakes'.

In this manner Loki is to lie bound until Ragnarok.

ODIN AND KING GEIRRØD

A king had two sons. One was called Agnar, the other Geirröd.
When Agnar was ten years old and Geirröd was eight, they rowed
out in a boat one day to go fishing. The wind drove them to sea.
In the darkness, their boat was dashed against land, and they went
up from the shore and met an old peasant and his wife. Here they
spent the winter. The old woman reared Agnar, and the old
fellow reared Geirröd. This old fellow and his wife were none
other than Odin and Frigg.

When spring came, the old fellow gave the boys a ship. He and
the old woman went down with them to the shore, and the old
fellow took Geirröd aside and talked with him. The winds were
favorable to the boys, and they came to their father's boathouse.
Geirröd stood in the bow of the ship. He sprang ashore, shoved
the ship out again, and shouted to his brother: "Now go where
the troll can take you!" But Geirröd went up to the hall, and there
they received him well. His father was dead now, and Geirröd was
made king and became a renowned man.

Odin and Frigg sat in Lidskjalv and looked out over the universe. "Do you see the way your foster son, Agnar, is living in a
cave with a troll hag," said Odin, "and having children with her?
While my foster son, Geirröd, is a king and rules over a realm."

"But he's so miserly," said Frigg, "that he tortures his guests
if he thinks too many have come."

Odin said this was a lie, and they made a wager about it.
Then Frigg sent her servant, Fulla, to Geirröd. The servant told

72

the king to beware of a sorcerer who had come to the land, and no doubt wanted to bewitch him. He would recognize this sorcerer by the fact that no dog, no matter how ferocious it was, would jump on him. It was only gossip that Geirröd was not hospitable. Nonetheless, he had the man seized on whom the dogs would not jump.

The man was clad in a blue cloak, and called himself *Grimne* (the mask). Otherwise, he did not tell anything more about himself, even though he was asked. The king wanted to make him talk, and started to torture him. He put him between two fires. There he sat for eight nights, and no one gave him anything to eat. King Geirröd had a son who was ten years old, and was called Agnar after his uncle. Agnar went over to Grimne and gave him a full horn to drink from. His father did wrong, he said, to torture a blameless man in this way. Grimne emptied the horn. The fire had now come so close that his cloak was singed.

Now Grimne talked for a long time. First he praised Agnar: "For a single drink, you shall never receive better thanks than I shall give you." Thereafter he described the thirteen realms of the gods. He told about food and drink and life in Valhall, and how large Valhall and Bilskirne were. He told of the goat, Heidrun, and the deer, *Eiktyrne,* and enumerated all the rivers of heaven and earth. He told of the horses on which the gods ride to council, of Yggdrasil, of the Valkyries, and the horses which draw the sun, of the wolves that rush after them, and how the world was created. Finally he named all the names by which he, himself, was known.

When he had finished, he turned to Geirröd and cried: "You are drunk, Geirröd! You have drunk too much. You have lost Odin's favor. I have told you much, but you remember only a little. Now your life is at an end. This is Odin you see here – approach me, if you can!"

King Geirröd was sitting with his sword across his knees. When he now heard that it was Odin who was sitting there, he

73

sprang up and wanted to take him away from the fire. The sword slipped out of his hand with the hilt downwards. The king's foot slipped, and he fell forward. The sword went through him, and this proved fatal.

But Agnar was king in the land, and reigned a long time afterwards.

ODIN AND THE SKALDIC MEAD

Kvase the Wise travelled far throughout the world, and taught mortals wisdom. Once he came to some dwarfs who were called *Fjalar* and *Galar*. They lured him along with them to a lonely spot, and killed him. They let his blood run down into two vats and a cauldron. They mingled honey with the blood, and it turned into a mead which was such that whoever drank of it became a *skald* or wiseman. The dwarfs told the Æsir that Kvase had drowned in his own wisdom.

Then the dwarfs invited a jotun named *Gilling* to visit them with his wife. They asked Gilling if he wanted to row out on the sea with them, and this he was willing to do. As they were going along the shore, the dwarfs rowed onto a rock and the boat turned over. Gilling could not swim, and drowned. But the dwarfs righted the boat and rowed to shore.

They told Gilling's wife what had happened, and she took it badly and cried aloud. Then Fjalar said that it might be easier for her if she went out and looked at the spot where her husband had drowned, and she had nothing against this. But to Galar, his brother, he said that he was to take a millstone up over the door, and drop it on her head when she went out — he was tired of her shrieking, he said. Galar did as his brother told him.

When *Suttung*, Gilling's son, heard of what had happened, he set out, and taking the dwarfs he went out to sea with them. He put them on a rock which stood under water at high tide. Now they were in danger of losing their lives. They begged Suttung for mercy, and offered him the precious mead as compensation for the slaying of his father and mother. He accepted the offer, and they came to terms. Suttung took the mead home with him, and hid it. He put his daughter, *Gunnlod,* to guard it.

When Odin heard of this, he set out from home and wanted to get hold of the mead. He came to a place where nine thralls were mowing. He asked if he should sharpen their scythes, and they were only too glad to let him. He took the whetstone from his belt, and sharpened the scythes. The thralls thought they cut exceedingly well afterwards, and asked if he wanted to sell the whetstone. He had nothing against this, and said that whoever wanted to buy it should just say so. But they were all eager to buy it. Then Odin threw the whetstone up in the air. They all tried to catch hold of it, and it ended with the thralls cutting each other's throats with the scythes.

Odin was given shelter for the night by a jotun named *Bauge.* He was Suttung's brother. Bauge complained that he was badly off. His nine thralls had killed each other, he said, and he did not know where he was going to get workers from. This time Odin called himself *Bolverk* (mischief-maker). He offered to do the work of nine men for Bauge, but as payment he demanded a drink of Suttung's mead. Bauge said that he had no control over the mead, for Suttung wanted to have it alone, but nonetheless he promised to go with Bolverk and try to get hold of it.

In the summer Bolverk did the work of nine men for Bauge. But, when winter set in, he asked for his wages. Then they both went to Suttung. Bauge told him what he and Bolverk had agreed upon, but Suttung crossly refused to let either of them have a single drop of the mead. Then Bolverk said to Bauge that they would have to resort to trickery in order to get hold of the mead, and Bauge agreed to help him. Bolverk then pulled out an auger and said that Bauge was to bore a hole through the mountain with it. Bauge started to bore, and after a while he said that now he had bored a hole through the mountain. But Bolverk blew into the hole made by the auger, and the chips

flew out at him. Then he knew that Bauge was thinking of betraying him, and said that he was to bore all the way through. Bauge bored anew, and when Bolverk blew again, the chips flew inwards. Then Bolverk turned himself into a serpent and slipped in through the auger hole. Bauge jabbed at him with the auger, but did not strike him.

Odin now went to the place where Gunnlod had hidden the mead, and was with her for three nights. Then she gave him permission to take three sips of the mead, and he drank it all up.

Then Odin put on an eagle's guise, and flew away as fast as he could. But when Suttung discovered the mead was gone, he turned himself into an eagle too, and set out after him. The Æsir saw Odin come flying, and put vats out in the yard. When Odin was inside the walls of Asgard, he spit the mead out into the vats. But Suttung was now so close behind him that he expelled some of the mead out backwards, and, as there was no one to catch it, anyone who wanted it could take it, and it became the lot of the poor skalds.

Odin gave Suttung's mead to the Æsir and to those men who can compose verse.

HÅRBARD AND TOR

As usual, Tor had been east fighting jotuns. On the way home he came to a sound, and on the other side stood the ferryman with the boat. Tor called over to him, and wanted to know his name. The ferryman did not reply to this, but shouted back that the one who was to be ferried would have to say his name.

"You'll have to ferry me over," said Tor, without replying to what he was asked about, "then you'll get something to eat from me. I have it in the basket on my back, and better food is not to be found. I, myself, ate my fill of both herring and oats before I left home and I'm not hungry yet."

"You talk of big-eating as though it were a man's work," said the ferryman. "But little do you know. There is sorrow at your home now because your mother is dead."

"What you're saying now," replied Tor, "is the biggest lie. My mother is not dead."

The ferryman now started taunting him: "You don't look as though you own three farms, the way you're standing there, barefoot and clad like a beggar. You look like you hardly own the pants you are wearing."

"Come here with the boat now," said Tor. "I'll show you the boat-landing. Or who owns the boat?"

"His name is *Hildolv*, and he lives in *Rådöysund*," replied the ferryman. "He said that I was only to ferry over people I knew, and, otherwise, only worthy folk, not all manner of rabble and horsethieves. If you want to come over, you'll have to tell me your name."

"I am the son of Odin and the father of Magne – you're talking to Tor now," replied the god proudly. "But now you'll have to tell me your name, too."

The ferryman, who was none other than Odin himself, said that he was called *Hårbard,* and added a few insults which showed that he was not the least bit impressed. This made Tor angry.

"If it weren't for the fact that my bundle would get wet if I waded over this sound, you vermin, you'd get the payment you deserved for such words," he shouted.

"Good! I'll stand here and wait for you," said Hårbard. "Ever since you fought with Rungne, you haven't met anyone as strong as I am."

"Yes, you remind me of Rungne," said Tor. "He had a head of stone, and still I felled him. What great deed were you performing then?"

"I spent five winters with Fjolvar on the island of *Allgrön,*" (Earth) said Hårbard. "There we fought and killed warriors, and had many adventures. What were you doing then, Tor?"

"I killed Tjatse, and threw his eyes up to heaven," said Tor. "What did you do?"

"With cunning, I lured the troll hags from their men," said Hårbard. "Lebard was a hard jotun. He gave me a magic staff, but I betrayed him so he went mad."

"Then you rewarded a good gift badly," said Tor.

"One oak keeps what is cut from the other," said Hårbard. "Everyone looks out for his own good. What were you doing?"

"I was east killing jotun women when they went into the mountain. For the jotun race would be too great if they were all allowed in live, and there would be few mortals in Midgard. But what were you doing then, Hårbard?"

"I was in Valland," replied Hårbard, "causing strife. I egged on the warriors, and never let them come to terms. Odin gets the earls that fall in battle, but Tor gets the thralls."

Tor said, "You'd probably administer things unequally among the Æsir if you had the power to."

Hårbard: "Tor is strong enough, but he has no courage. You were scared to death when you squeezed yourself into the glove. Neither dared you to cough nor sneeze, you were so afraid that the jotun would hear you."

Tor: "Hårbard, you wretch, I'd kill you if only I could come over the sound!"

Hårbard: "Why should you come over the sound? It's not at all necessary. But tell me what you did next."

Tor: "I was east defending the boundary river, and Svårang's sons came against me and trew stones. But they were not victorious, for they had to beg me for peace. What did you do then?"

Hårbard: "I was also in the east. There I was trifling with the maid as white as linen, and she liked me well."

"I slew the berserker women on Læsöy," said Tor. "They had done the most terrible things they could, bewitching people from their senses."

"That was badly done, Tor, to slay womenfolk."

"They were werewolves," said Tor, "not women. They tore down my ship which I had propped up, threatened me with crowbars, and chased Tjalve away. What were you doing at that time?"

"I was in the army, which gathered here to color its spears red," said Hårbard.

"Then it was you who offered us such hard terms?" asked Tor.

"I'll pay forfeit with arm-rings," said Hårbard.

Tor: "Where have you learned such biting jeers? I've never heard anything like it in all my life!"

"From the old fellows who dwell in the home-mounds," said Hårbard.

"A good name you give to the burial mounds," said Tor. "But you'll sorely regret these taunts if I wade across the sound. You'll howl worse than a wolf if I hit you with my hammer."

"Siv has a man at home with her!" jeered Hårbard. "I guess you'd be glad to meet him! You'll have to prove your strength against him."

"You say what you think will hurt me most," said Tor, "but your throat is full of lies!"

"But I've delayed you on your journey," said Hårbard. "You could have been a long way by now."

"Yes, you've held me up, you wretch," said Tor.

"But never did I think that Tor the Charioteer would let himself be held up by a goatherd," said Hårbard.

"Now I'll give you some good advice," said Tor. "Row over here with the boat, and let us put an end to this quarrelling."

Hårbard: "Go away from the sound, for I'm not ferrying you over."

"Then tell me the way," asked Tor, "as long as you won't put me over."

"It's a long journey," said Hårbard, "first a way to the stock and then a way to the stone, then you turn to the left and you'll come to Verland. There you'll find your mother, and she'll show you the way to Odin's realm."

"Will I get there today?" asked Tor.

"With toils and struggles you might be there by the time the sun rises tomorrow morning," said Hårbard.

"Now our talk will end," said Tor. "You deal only in quarrels, but I'll pay you for it if we meet another time."

"Go where the troll takes you!" shouted Hårbard after him.

RAGNAROK

The whole world, with gods and mortals, will go under one day in *Ragnarok,* the "Twilight of the Gods".

The gods know in advance when it is going to occur, for many warnings and signs indicate that the portentous events are drawin nigh. In Asgard the rooster *Gyllenkambe* (Golden Comb) awakens the heroes with Odin in Valhall. In Jotunheim the red rooster *Fjalar* crows, and simultaneously Hel's sooty rooster starts to crow. Outside Gnipahelleren, Garm howls terribly. Then come three years of hard battles over the whole world. Evil and violence reign, brother slays brother for the sake of gain, and the son does not spare his own father, nor the father his own son. It is the time of the axe and the sword, the time of the wind and the wolf, before the world is destroyed. When these three years are over, the *Fimbul Winter* (the great winter) will set in. Then snow blows from every direction, the winds howl, and the sun is unable to shine and bring warmth. Three such winters will come, one after the other, and there will be no summers in between.

The wolves devour the Sun and the Moon, blood spouts over the heavens and fills the air, and the stars disappear. The whole earth and all the mountains tremble, and the trees are loosened. Mountains fall, and every bond is broken or worn through.

The Fenris Wolf comes loose, and the sea pours in over the shores in great billows, for the Serpent of Midgard writhes in fury and wants to come up on land. The ship *Naglfar* tears itself loose in this swell. It is made of the nails of dead mortals. The ship comes sailing from the north. Loki steers, and all of Hel's

mighty host of the dead are on board. From the east the army of
frost giants pours forth, with the jotun *Rym* as its leader. The
Fenris Wolf rushes forth with gaping jaws. Its lower jaw is
down on the earth, and the upper jaw touches the vault of the
heavens, and it could have gaped even higher had there been

room for it. Fire flashes from its eyes and nostrils. The Serpent of Midgard goes alongside the wolf. It spouts venom out over the earth and sea, and is terrible to behold. In this din the heavens are torn asunder, and the Sons of Muspell come riding forth. They come from the south, and Surt rides foremost with fire burning all around him. His sword shines brighter than the sun. But when they ride out on Bivrost, it breaks beneath them.

The Sons of Muspell make their way to the Plain of Vigrid, and here, too, come the Fenris Wolf and the Serpent of Midgard, Rym with the frost giants, and Loki with his company from Hel. The Sons of Muspell array themselves for battle in a battalion by themselves, and their weapons shine from afar.

But when this happens, the god Heimdall stands up and blows piercing blasts on Gjallarhorn, and awakens all the gods. They hold council and confer. Odin rides to Mimesbrunn, and seeks advice for himself and his warriors. Then Yggdrasil shudders, the old tree sighs complainingly, and everyone on earth and in heaven is filled with dread. The Æsir and the fallen heroes gird themselves for battle and seize their weapons. Then they set out for the Plain of Vigrid. Odin rides first wearing his golden helmet and beautiful coat of mail, and carrying the spear Gungne. He heads for the Fenris Wolf. By his side goes Tor, but he cannot help him for he has enough to do with the Serpent of Midgard. Frey heads towards Surt, Ty goes towards Hel's dog Garm, which has now come loose, and Heimdall goes to do battle with Loki.

Between Frey and Surt there is a hard struggle before Frey falls. The loss of the good sword that he gave to Skirne proves fatal. Ty and Garm slay one another. Similarly, Heimdall and Loki kill each other. Tor slays the Serpent of Midgard. But after the battle he takes but nine steps forward, and then falls dead to the ground from all the venom which the Serpent has blown at him. The wolf devours Odin, and this is the end of the god; but immediately afterwards Vidar strides forward. He places one

84

foot on the wolf's lower jaw and, taking the upper jaw with his hands, he wrenches the jaw to bits. On his foot Vidar has a shoe which is made of those bits of hide which people cut off their shoes at the toes and heels. Thus one should always throw such pieces away so they can be of aid to the Æsir.

Surt casts fire over the earth and burns all things. Everything is destroyed. The earth sinks into the sea. The flames splutter, and smoke and steam billow up. Everything turns black, while the heat beats high against the heavenly vault.

A NEW EARTH

A new earth rises up out of the sea. It is green and fair, and there the grain grows on unsown fields.

> *Waterfalls flow,*
> *The eagle flies above*
> *The one on the mountain*
> *Who catches the fish.*

The new sun drives across the heavens, big and radiant.

Vidar and Våle live, and the world conflagration has not harmed them. They set up housekeeping on Idavollen where Asgard stood before. Tor's sons, Mode and Magne, also come there, and they have Mjölne with them. Balder and Hod come home from Hel, and Höne comes back from Vanaheim. They all sit down and talk together, and reminise over what happened in the days of old. Then in the grass they find the golden pieces which the Æsir owned long ago, and they play at tables together.

The two mortals, who have remained hidden and subsisted on the morning dew, now come forth, and from them stem new races of mankind who shall dwell on the new earth. There is no sorrow, no want and no evil, only joy and innocence. In *Gimle* stands a hall fairer than the sun, and covered with gold. There guiltless crowds shall build and dwell, and enjoy everlasting happiness.

> *Then the Almighty*
> *Comes to reign,*
> *The strong from above*
> *Who rules over everything.*